This Party Planner Belongs to:

Contents

Party Planner
and
Event Organizer Notebook

Staying Party Organized is a key to the smooth running of the party, whether you have a small immediate family or a large extended family.

With kids, there are always celebrations, presents with teachers, birthday parties, games and plays, cooking, baking, and other fun to keep up with each holiday, not just a Christmas, Halloween, or Thanksgiving.

This party planner provides all you need to get the pressure and uncertainty out of holidays. Even it's just your kids' birthday party at home or a big event that needs to be planed all well.

Like an Event Organizer Checklist or Task List Tracker, this Party Planner Book will help you stay in control and make your party as smooth as you ever imagine.

So, let's get organized!

Valentine C.

Party Plan Overview

DETAILS

Date / Time

Theme / Colors

Location

GUESTS

PARTY SCHEDULE

MENU IDEA

ACTIVITIES PLAN

DECORATING IDEA

Table

Room

Outdoor Decorations

NOTES

NOTES

NOTES

Monthly Planner

MONTH OF: ....

SUNDAY	MONDAY	TUESDAY	WEDNESDAY	THURSDAY	FRIDAY	SATURDAY

NOTES

....

....

....

....

....

....

Monthly Planner

MONTH OF: ....

SUNDAY	MONDAY	TUESDAY	WEDNESDAY	THURSDAY	FRIDAY	SATURDAY

NOTES

....

....

....

....

....

....

Monthly Planner

MONTH OF: ....

SUNDAY	MONDAY	TUESDAY	WEDNESDAY	THURSDAY	FRIDAY	SATURDAY

NOTES

....

....

....

....

....

....

Monthly Planner

MONTH OF: ....

SUNDAY	MONDAY	TUESDAY	WEDNESDAY	THURSDAY	FRIDAY	SATURDAY

NOTES

Monthly Planner

MONTH OF: ....

SUNDAY	MONDAY	TUESDAY	WEDNESDAY	THURSDAY	FRIDAY	SATURDAY

NOTES

Monthly Planner

MONTH OF: ....

SUNDAY	MONDAY	TUESDAY	WEDNESDAY	THURSDAY	FRIDAY	SATURDAY

NOTES

Monthly Planner

MONTH OF: ....

SUNDAY	MONDAY	TUESDAY	WEDNESDAY	THURSDAY	FRIDAY	SATURDAY

NOTES

....

....

....

....

....

....

Monthly Planner

MONTH OF: ....

SUNDAY	MONDAY	TUESDAY	WEDNESDAY	THURSDAY	FRIDAY	SATURDAY

NOTES

....

....

....

....

....

....

Monthly Planner

MONTH OF: ....

SUNDAY	MONDAY	TUESDAY	WEDNESDAY	THURSDAY	FRIDAY	SATURDAY

NOTES

....
....
....
....
....
....

Monthly Planner

MONTH OF: ....

SUNDAY	MONDAY	TUESDAY	WEDNESDAY	THURSDAY	FRIDAY	SATURDAY

NOTES

....

....

....

....

....

....

Monthly Planner

MONTH OF: ....

SUNDAY	MONDAY	TUESDAY	WEDNESDAY	THURSDAY	FRIDAY	SATURDAY

NOTES

....

....

....

....

....

Monthly Planner

MONTH OF: ....

SUNDAY	MONDAY	TUESDAY	WEDNESDAY	THURSDAY	FRIDAY	SATURDAY

NOTES

....

....

....

....

....

....

Things To Do

2-3 WEEKS BEFORE

☐ ....
☐ ....
☐ ....
☐ ....
☐ ....
☐ ....
☐ ....
☐ ....
☐ ....
☐ ....
☐ ....
☐ ....
☐ ....
☐ ....
☐ ....

Tips

● When menu planning, ask guests to bring some of the dishes. This will make your job easier.

● Place gather and recipes with your Party Planner.

● Purchase household goods like toilet paper, paper towels, napkins, Kleenex, dish soap, and hand soap.

● Purchase additional kitchenware needed such as plates, bowls, spoons, slow cookers, and pitchers.

NOTES

1 WEEK BEFORE

☐ ....
☐ ....
☐ ....
☐ ....
☐ ....
☐ ....
☐ ....
☐ ....
☐ ....
☐ ....
☐ ....
☐ ....
☐ ....
☐ ....
☐ ....

Tips

● Clean out the fridge / freezer / pantry to make space and see what items are missing or expired.

● Make sure to buy enough food per person unless you want leftovers or are big eaters then increase a little more.

NOTES

NOTES

Things To Do

2-3 DAYS BEFORE

- [ ] ....
- [ ] ....
- [ ] ....
- [ ] ....
- [ ] ....
- [ ] ....
- [ ] ....
- [ ] ....
- [ ] ....
- [ ] ....
- [ ] ....
- [ ] ....
- [ ] ....
- [ ] ....

DAY BEFORE

- [ ] ....
- [ ] ....
- [ ] ....
- [ ] ....
- [ ] ....
- [ ] ....
- [ ] ....
- [ ] ....
- [ ] ....
- [ ] ....
- [ ] ....
- [ ] ....
- [ ] ....
- [ ] ....

Tips

- Last minute tidying will still need to be done but the majority of cleaning can be done in advance.

- Set up extra tables and chairs after cleaning. If you don't have folding tables and chairs, borrow them from friends or relatives.

- Grocery stores are super busy! Early in the morning or late at night to avoid the biggest crowds.

NOTES

Tips

- Pulling ingredients ahead of. It will let you know if you forgot anything.

- Bake the bakery (if any) and store at room temp or in fridge according to recipe instructions.

- Store veggies in the zip-top plastic bags in fridge.

- Set up extra tables and chairs after cleaning. If you don't have folding tables and chairs, borrow them from friends or relatives.

- Take each recipe and put it on the counter with the accompanying baking dish / pot / pan and any non-perishable ingredients.

Everything will be ready for tomorrow!

NOTES

Things To Do

The Day of Event

NOTES

Invitation Cards & Poster

THEME

Colors:

Patterns:

Descriptions:

IDEA & MOCK UP

Menu Planner

Menu	Ingredients
Appetizer	
Main Course	
Side Dishes	
Desserts	
Beverages	

Groceries Lists

Name of Recipe

Oven Temp: .... **Cooking Time:** .... **Serves:** .... **From:** ....

Ingredients

- ☐ ....
- ☐ ....
- ☐ ....
- ☐ ....
- ☐ ....
- ☐ ....

- ☐ ....
- ☐ ....
- ☐ ....
- ☐ ....
- ☐ ....
- ☐ ....

- ☐ ....
- ☐ ....
- ☐ ....
- ☐ ....
- ☐ ....
- ☐ ....

Directions

....
....
....
....
....
....
....
....
....
....
....
....
....
....

Notes

....
....
....

Name of Recipe

Oven Temp: .... **Cooking Time:** .... **Serves:** .... **From:** ....

Ingredients

- [ ]
- [ ]
- [ ]
- [ ]
- [ ]
- [ ]

- [ ]
- [ ]
- [ ]
- [ ]
- [ ]
- [ ]

- [ ]
- [ ]
- [ ]
- [ ]
- [ ]
- [ ]

Directions

Notes

Name of Recipe

Oven Temp: .... **Cooking Time:** .... **Serves:** .... **From:** ....

Ingredients

- ☐ ....
- ☐ ....
- ☐ ....
- ☐ ....
- ☐ ....

- ☐ ....
- ☐ ....
- ☐ ....
- ☐ ....
- ☐ ....
- ☐ ....

- ☐ ....
- ☐ ....
- ☐ ....
- ☐ ....
- ☐ ....
- ☐ ....

Directions

....

....

....

....

....

....

....

....

....

....

....

....

....

....

....

Notes

....

....

....

Oven Temp: .... **Cooking Time:** .... **Serves:** .... **From:** ....

Ingredients

- ☐ ....
- ☐ ....
- ☐ ....
- ☐ ....
- ☐ ....
- ☐ ....

- ☐ ....
- ☐ ....
- ☐ ....
- ☐ ....
- ☐ ....
- ☐ ....

- ☐ ....
- ☐ ....
- ☐ ....
- ☐ ....
- ☐ ....
- ☐ ....

Directions

....

....

....

....

....

....

....

....

....

....

....

....

....

....

Notes

....

....

Name of Recipe

Oven Temp: .... **Cooking Time:** .... **Serves:** .... **From:** ....

Ingredients

- [ ] ....
- [ ] ....
- [ ] ....
- [ ] ....
- [ ] ....
- [ ] ....

- [ ] ....
- [ ] ....
- [ ] ....
- [ ] ....
- [ ] ....
- [ ] ....

- [ ] ....
- [ ] ....
- [ ] ....
- [ ] ....
- [ ] ....
- [ ] ....

Directions

....
....
....
....
....
....
....
....
....
....
....
....
....
....

Notes

....
....
....

Name of Recipe

Oven Temp: _____ Cooking Time: _____ Serves: _____ From: _____

Ingredients

- [ ]
- [ ]
- [ ]
- [ ]
- [ ]
- [ ]
- [ ]

- [ ]
- [ ]
- [ ]
- [ ]
- [ ]
- [ ]
- [ ]

- [ ]
- [ ]
- [ ]
- [ ]
- [ ]
- [ ]
- [ ]

Directions

Notes

Name of Recipe

Oven Temp: .... Cooking Time: .... Serves: .... From: ....

Ingredients

☐ ....
☐ ....
☐ ....
☐ ....
☐ ....
☐ ....

☐ ....
☐ ....
☐ ....
☐ ....
☐ ....
☐ ....

☐ ....
☐ ....
☐ ....
☐ ....
☐ ....
☐ ....

Directions

Notes

Name of Recipe

Oven Temp: .... **Cooking Time:** .... **Serves:** .... **From:** ....

Ingredients

- [ ] ....
- [ ] ....
- [ ] ....
- [ ] ....
- [ ] ....
- [ ] ....

- [ ] ....
- [ ] ....
- [ ] ....
- [ ] ....
- [ ] ....
- [ ] ....

- [ ] ....
- [ ] ....
- [ ] ....
- [ ] ....
- [ ] ....
- [ ] ....

Directions

....

....

....

....

....

....

....

....

....

....

....

....

....

Notes

....

....

Name of Recipe

Oven Temp: _____ Cooking Time: _____ Serves: _____ From: _____

Ingredients

☐ _____ ☐ _____ ☐ _____
☐ _____ ☐ _____ ☐ _____
☐ _____ ☐ _____ ☐ _____
☐ _____ ☐ _____ ☐ _____
☐ _____ ☐ _____ ☐ _____
☐ _____ ☐ _____ ☐ _____

Directions

_____
_____
_____
_____
_____
_____
_____
_____
_____
_____
_____
_____
_____
_____
_____

Notes

_____
_____

 # Cooking Schedules

TIME	DISHES	NOTES
5 AM		
6 AM		
7 AM		
8 AM		
9 AM		
10 AM		
11 AM		
12 PM		
1 PM		
2 PM		
3 PM		
4 PM		
5 PM		
6 PM		
7 PM		

Theme & Decorations

THEME ELEMENTS

Colors:

Patterns & Textures:

Décor must have:

MAIN IDEAS

TABLE DECORATIONS

Party Decoration lists

ITEMS NEEDED	FOR	AMOUNT	Own	Buy	Borrow	NOTES
			☐	☐	☐	
			☐	☐	☐	
			☐	☐	☐	
			☐	☐	☐	
			☐	☐	☐	
			☐	☐	☐	
			☐	☐	☐	
			☐	☐	☐	
			☐	☐	☐	
			☐	☐	☐	
			☐	☐	☐	
			☐	☐	☐	
			☐	☐	☐	
			☐	☐	☐	
			☐	☐	☐	
			☐	☐	☐	
			☐	☐	☐	
			☐	☐	☐	
			☐	☐	☐	
			☐	☐	☐	
			☐	☐	☐	
			☐	☐	☐	
			☐	☐	☐	
			☐	☐	☐	
			☐	☐	☐	
			☐	☐	☐	
			☐	☐	☐	
			☐	☐	☐	

NOTES

NOTES

Activities & Entertainments

ACTIVITY'S NAME :	PERSON IN CHARGE :				
Details	**Items Needed**	**Own**	**Buy**	**Borrow**	**Notes**
		☐	☐	☐	
		☐	☐	☐	
		☐	☐	☐	
		☐	☐	☐	
		☐	☐	☐	
		☐	☐	☐	
		☐	☐	☐	

ACTIVITY'S NAME :	PERSON IN CHARGE :				
Details	**Items Needed**	**Own**	**Buy**	**Borrow**	**Notes**
		☐	☐	☐	
		☐	☐	☐	
		☐	☐	☐	
		☐	☐	☐	
		☐	☐	☐	
		☐	☐	☐	
		☐	☐	☐	

ACTIVITY'S NAME :	PERSON IN CHARGE :				
Details	**Items Needed**	**Own**	**Buy**	**Borrow**	**Notes**
		☐	☐	☐	
		☐	☐	☐	
		☐	☐	☐	
		☐	☐	☐	
		☐	☐	☐	
		☐	☐	☐	
		☐	☐	☐	

Activities & Entertainments

ACTIVITY'S NAME :   **PERSON IN CHARGE :**

Details	Items Needed	Own	Buy	Borrow	Notes
		☐	☐	☐	
		☐	☐	☐	
		☐	☐	☐	
		☐	☐	☐	
		☐	☐	☐	
		☐	☐	☐	
		☐	☐	☐	

ACTIVITY'S NAME :   **PERSON IN CHARGE :**

Details	Items Needed	Own	Buy	Borrow	Notes
		☐	☐	☐	
		☐	☐	☐	
		☐	☐	☐	
		☐	☐	☐	
		☐	☐	☐	
		☐	☐	☐	
		☐	☐	☐	

ACTIVITY'S NAME :   **PERSON IN CHARGE :**

Details	Items Needed	Own	Buy	Borrow	Notes
		☐	☐	☐	
		☐	☐	☐	
		☐	☐	☐	
		☐	☐	☐	
		☐	☐	☐	
		☐	☐	☐	

Activities & Entertainments

ACTIVITY'S NAME :   **PERSON IN CHARGE :**

Details	Items Needed	Own	Buy	Borrow	Notes
		☐	☐	☐	
		☐	☐	☐	
		☐	☐	☐	
		☐	☐	☐	
		☐	☐	☐	
		☐	☐	☐	
		☐	☐	☐	

ACTIVITY'S NAME :   **PERSON IN CHARGE :**

Details	Items Needed	Own	Buy	Borrow	Notes
		☐	☐	☐	
		☐	☐	☐	
		☐	☐	☐	
		☐	☐	☐	
		☐	☐	☐	
		☐	☐	☐	
		☐	☐	☐	

ACTIVITY'S NAME :   **PERSON IN CHARGE :**

Details	Items Needed	Own	Buy	Borrow	Notes
		☐	☐	☐	
		☐	☐	☐	
		☐	☐	☐	
		☐	☐	☐	
		☐	☐	☐	
		☐	☐	☐	
		☐	☐	☐	

Party Timeline

TIME	ACTIVITY	DESCRIPTIONS

PRIZES & ITEMS TO BUY	AMOUNT	BUDGET
☐		
☐		
☐		
☐		
☐		
☐		
☐		
☐		
☐		
☐		
☐		
☐		
☐		
☐		

NOTES

NOTES

NOTES

Shopping Lists

Store:

- ☐ --
- ☐ --
- ☐ --
- ☐ --
- ☐ --
- ☐ --
- ☐ --
- ☐ --

Store:

- ☐ --
- ☐ --
- ☐ --
- ☐ --
- ☐ --
- ☐ --
- ☐ --
- ☐ --

Store:

- ☐ --
- ☐ --
- ☐ --
- ☐ --
- ☐ --
- ☐ --
- ☐ --
- ☐ --

Store:

- ☐ --
- ☐ --
- ☐ --
- ☐ --
- ☐ --
- ☐ --
- ☐ --
- ☐ --

Store:

- ☐ --
- ☐ --
- ☐ --
- ☐ --
- ☐ --
- ☐ --
- ☐ --
- ☐ --

Store:

- ☐ --
- ☐ --
- ☐ --
- ☐ --
- ☐ --
- ☐ --
- ☐ --
- ☐ --

Shopping Lists

Store:

- [ ]
- [ ]
- [ ]
- [ ]
- [ ]
- [ ]
- [ ]
- [ ]

Store:

- [ ]
- [ ]
- [ ]
- [ ]
- [ ]
- [ ]
- [ ]
- [ ]

Store:

- [ ]
- [ ]
- [ ]
- [ ]
- [ ]
- [ ]
- [ ]
- [ ]

Store:

- [ ]
- [ ]
- [ ]
- [ ]
- [ ]
- [ ]
- [ ]
- [ ]

Store:

- [ ]
- [ ]
- [ ]
- [ ]
- [ ]
- [ ]
- [ ]
- [ ]

Store:

- [ ]
- [ ]
- [ ]
- [ ]
- [ ]
- [ ]
- [ ]
- [ ]

Shopping Lists

Store:

Store:

Store:

Store:

Store:

Store:

Shopping Lists

Store:

- ☐
- ☐
- ☐
- ☐
- ☐
- ☐
- ☐
- ☐

Store:

- ☐
- ☐
- ☐
- ☐
- ☐
- ☐
- ☐
- ☐

Store:

- ☐
- ☐
- ☐
- ☐
- ☐
- ☐
- ☐
- ☐

Store:

- ☐
- ☐
- ☐
- ☐
- ☐
- ☐
- ☐
- ☐

Store:

- ☐
- ☐
- ☐
- ☐
- ☐
- ☐
- ☐
- ☐

Store:

- ☐
- ☐
- ☐
- ☐
- ☐
- ☐
- ☐
- ☐

 # Shopping Lists

Store:

- ☐ --
- ☐ --
- ☐ --
- ☐ --
- ☐ --
- ☐ --
- ☐ --
- ☐ --

Store:

- ☐ --
- ☐ --
- ☐ --
- ☐ --
- ☐ --
- ☐ --
- ☐ --
- ☐ --

Store:

- ☐ --
- ☐ --
- ☐ --
- ☐ --
- ☐ --
- ☐ --
- ☐ --
- ☐ --

Store:

- ☐ --
- ☐ --
- ☐ --
- ☐ --
- ☐ --
- ☐ --
- ☐ --
- ☐ --

Store:

- ☐ --
- ☐ --
- ☐ --
- ☐ --
- ☐ --
- ☐ --
- ☐ --
- ☐ --

Store:

- ☐ --
- ☐ --
- ☐ --
- ☐ --
- ☐ --
- ☐ --
- ☐ --
- ☐ --

Shopping Lists

Store:

- [ ]
- [ ]
- [ ]
- [ ]
- [ ]
- [ ]
- [ ]
- [ ]

Store:

- [ ]
- [ ]
- [ ]
- [ ]
- [ ]
- [ ]
- [ ]
- [ ]

Store:

- [ ]
- [ ]
- [ ]
- [ ]
- [ ]
- [ ]
- [ ]
- [ ]

Store:

- [ ]
- [ ]
- [ ]
- [ ]
- [ ]
- [ ]
- [ ]
- [ ]

Store:

- [ ]
- [ ]
- [ ]
- [ ]
- [ ]
- [ ]
- [ ]
- [ ]

Store:

- [ ]
- [ ]
- [ ]
- [ ]
- [ ]
- [ ]
- [ ]
- [ ]

Party Guest List

GUEST	RSVP	BRINGING	REQUESTS	ADULT	KIDS	NOTES
				☐	☐	
				☐	☐	
				☐	☐	
				☐	☐	
				☐	☐	
				☐	☐	
				☐	☐	
				☐	☐	
				☐	☐	
				☐	☐	
				☐	☐	
				☐	☐	
				☐	☐	
				☐	☐	
				☐	☐	
				☐	☐	
				☐	☐	
				☐	☐	
				☐	☐	
				☐	☐	
				☐	☐	
				☐	☐	
				☐	☐	
				☐	☐	
				☐	☐	
				☐	☐	
				☐	☐	
				☐	☐	

Party Guest List

GUEST	RSVP	BRINGING	REQUESTS	ADULT	KIDS	NOTES
				☐	☐	
				☐	☐	
				☐	☐	
				☐	☐	
				☐	☐	
				☐	☐	
				☐	☐	
				☐	☐	
				☐	☐	
				☐	☐	
				☐	☐	
				☐	☐	
				☐	☐	
				☐	☐	
				☐	☐	
				☐	☐	
				☐	☐	
				☐	☐	
				☐	☐	
				☐	☐	
				☐	☐	
				☐	☐	
				☐	☐	
				☐	☐	
				☐	☐	
				☐	☐	
				☐	☐	

Party Guest List

GUEST	RSVP	BRINGING	REQUESTS	ADULT	KIDS	NOTES
				☐	☐	
				☐	☐	
				☐	☐	
				☐	☐	
				☐	☐	
				☐	☐	
				☐	☐	
				☐	☐	
				☐	☐	
				☐	☐	
				☐	☐	
				☐	☐	
				☐	☐	
				☐	☐	
				☐	☐	
				☐	☐	
				☐	☐	
				☐	☐	
				☐	☐	
				☐	☐	
				☐	☐	
				☐	☐	
				☐	☐	
				☐	☐	
				☐	☐	
				☐	☐	
				☐	☐	

Party Guest List

GUEST	RSVP	BRINGING	REQUESTS	ADULT	KIDS	NOTES
				☐	☐	
				☐	☐	
				☐	☐	
				☐	☐	
				☐	☐	
				☐	☐	
				☐	☐	
				☐	☐	
				☐	☐	
				☐	☐	
				☐	☐	
				☐	☐	
				☐	☐	
				☐	☐	
				☐	☐	
				☐	☐	
				☐	☐	
				☐	☐	
				☐	☐	
				☐	☐	
				☐	☐	
				☐	☐	
				☐	☐	
				☐	☐	
				☐	☐	
				☐	☐	
				☐	☐	
				☐	☐	
				☐	☐	

Cards to Send

NAME: **SENT:** ◯

Address   Note

NAME: **SENT:** ◯

Address   Note

NAME: **SENT:** ◯

Address   Note

NAME: **SENT:** ◯

Address   Note

NAME: **SENT:** ◯

Address   Note

NAME: **SENT:** ◯

Address   Note

NAME: **SENT:** ◯

Address   Note

NAME: **SENT:** ◯

Address   Note

NAME: **SENT:** ◯

Address   Note

NAME: **SENT:** ◯

Address   Note

Cards to Send

NAME: **SENT:** ◯

Note

Address ....

....

....

....

NAME: **SENT:** ◯

Note

Address ....

....

....

....

NAME: **SENT:** ◯

Note

Address ....

....

....

....

NAME: **SENT:** ◯

Note

Address ....

....

....

....

NAME: **SENT:** ◯

Note

Address ....

....

....

....

NAME: **SENT:** ◯

Note

Address ....

....

....

....

NAME: **SENT:** ◯

Note

Address ....

....

....

....

NAME: **SENT:** ◯

Note

Address ....

....

....

....

NAME: **SENT:** ◯

Note

Address ....

....

....

....

NAME: **SENT:** ◯

Note

Address ....

....

....

....

Cards to Send

NAME: **SENT:** ◯

Address ---------------------------

Note

NAME: **SENT:** ◯

Address ---------------------------

Note

NAME: **SENT:** ◯

Address ---------------------------

Note

NAME: **SENT:** ◯

Address ---------------------------

Note

NAME: **SENT:** ◯

Address ---------------------------

Note

NAME: **SENT:** ◯

Address ---------------------------

Note

NAME: **SENT:** ◯

Address ---------------------------

Note

NAME: **SENT:** ◯

Address ---------------------------

Note

NAME: **SENT:** ◯

Address ---------------------------

Note

NAME: **SENT:** ◯

Address ---------------------------

Note

Cards to Send

NAME: SENT: ○

Address ....

Note

....

....

....

NAME: SENT: ○

Address ....

Note

....

....

....

NAME: SENT: ○

Address ....

Note

....

....

....

NAME: SENT: ○

Address ....

Note

....

....

....

NAME: SENT: ○

Address ....

Note

....

....

....

NAME: SENT: ○

Address ....

Note

....

....

....

NAME: SENT: ○

Address ....

Note

....

....

....

NAME: SENT: ○

Address ....

Note

....

....

....

NAME: SENT: ○

Address ....

Note

....

....

....

NAME: SENT: ○

Address ....

Note

....

....

....

Cards to Send

NAME: **SENT:** ◯

Address ....

Note

....

....

....

NAME: **SENT:** ◯

Address ....

Note

....

....

....

NAME: **SENT:** ◯

Address ....

Note

....

....

....

NAME: **SENT:** ◯

Address ....

Note

....

....

....

NAME: **SENT:** ◯

Address ....

Note

....

....

....

NAME: **SENT:** ◯

Address ....

Note

....

....

....

NAME: **SENT:** ◯

Address ....

Note

....

....

....

NAME: **SENT:** ◯

Address ....

Note

....

....

....

NAME: **SENT:** ◯

Address ....

Note

....

....

....

NAME: **SENT:** ◯

Address ....

Note

....

....

....

Cards to Send

NAME: **SENT:** ◯

Address ....

Note

....

....

....

NAME: **SENT:** ◯

Address ....

Note

....

....

....

NAME: **SENT:** ◯

Address ....

Note

....

....

....

NAME: **SENT:** ◯

Address ....

Note

....

....

....

NAME: **SENT:** ◯

Address ....

Note

....

....

....

NAME: **SENT:** ◯

Address ....

Note

....

....

....

NAME: **SENT:** ◯

Address ....

Note

....

....

....

NAME: **SENT:** ◯

Address ....

Note

....

....

....

NAME: **SENT:** ◯

Address ....

Note

....

....

....

NAME: **SENT:** ◯

Address ....

Note

....

....

....

Party Budget Tracker

Date	Item	Description	Category	Estimated	Actual

Party Budget Tracker

Date	Item	Description	Category	Estimated	Actual

Total Budget

Category					
Budget					
Spend					

Important Contacts

NAME:

BUSINESS:

PHONE:

FAX:

NOTES:

NAME:

BUSINESS:

PHONE:

FAX:

NOTES:

NAME:

BUSINESS:

PHONE:

FAX:

NOTES:

NAME:

BUSINESS:

PHONE:

FAX:

NOTES:

NAME:

BUSINESS:

PHONE:

FAX:

NOTES:

NAME:

BUSINESS:

PHONE:

FAX:

NOTES:

NAME:

BUSINESS:

PHONE:

FAX:

NOTES:

NAME:

BUSINESS:

PHONE:

FAX:

NOTES:

Important Contacts

NAME:

BUSINESS:

PHONE:

FAX:

NOTES:

NAME:

BUSINESS:

PHONE:

FAX:

NOTES:

NAME:

BUSINESS:

PHONE:

FAX:

NOTES:

NAME:

BUSINESS:

PHONE:

FAX:

NOTES:

NAME:

BUSINESS:

PHONE:

FAX:

NOTES:

NAME:

BUSINESS:

PHONE:

FAX:

NOTES:

NAME:

BUSINESS:

PHONE:

FAX:

NOTES:

NAME:

BUSINESS:

PHONE:

FAX:

NOTES:

Important Contacts

NAME:

BUSINESS:

PHONE:

FAX:

NOTES:

NAME:

BUSINESS:

PHONE:

FAX:

NOTES:

NAME:

BUSINESS:

PHONE:

FAX:

NOTES:

NAME:

BUSINESS:

PHONE:

FAX:

NOTES:

NAME:

BUSINESS:

PHONE:

FAX:

NOTES:

NAME:

BUSINESS:

PHONE:

FAX:

NOTES:

NAME:

BUSINESS:

PHONE:

FAX:

NOTES:

NAME:

BUSINESS:

PHONE:

FAX:

NOTES:

Important Contacts

NAME:

BUSINESS:

PHONE:

FAX:

NOTES:

NAME:

BUSINESS:

PHONE:

FAX:

NOTES:

NAME:

BUSINESS:

PHONE:

FAX:

NOTES:

NAME:

BUSINESS:

PHONE:

FAX:

NOTES:

NAME:

BUSINESS:

PHONE:

FAX:

NOTES:

NAME:

BUSINESS:

PHONE:

FAX:

NOTES:

NAME:

BUSINESS:

PHONE:

FAX:

NOTES:

NAME:

BUSINESS:

PHONE:

FAX:

NOTES:

NOTES

NOTES

NOTES

Made in United States
Troutdale, OR
08/23/2023

12328019R10046